Handy South Carolina Genealogy Handbook

by Gary L. Morris

ISBN-13: 978-1506176703

ISBN-10: 1506176704

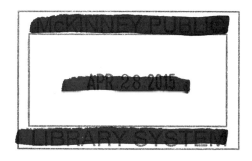

Table of Contents

Notes

Genealogical Research in South Carolina

As one of the original thirteen colonies, there are many historical and genealogical records and resources available for tracing your family history in South Carolina. Because there are so many records held at many different locations, tracking down the records for your ancestor can be an ominous task. Don't worry though, we know just where they are, and we'll show you which records you'll need, while helping you to understand:

1. What they are
2. Where to find them
3. How to use them

These records can be found both online and off, so we'll introduce you to online websites, indexes and databases, as well as brick-and-mortar repositories and other institutions that will help with your research in South Carolina. So that you will have a more comprehensive understanding of these records, we have provided a brief history of the "Palmetto State" to illustrate what type of records may have been generated during specific time periods. That information will assist you in pinpointing times and locations on which to focus the search for your South Carolina ancestors and their records.

A Brief History of South Carolina

Several Indian groups populated the region before European settlement, notably the Cherokee and others of Iroquoian stock, the Catawba, and those of Muskogean blood. Spanish sailors explored the area in the sixteenth century and unsuccessfully attempted to establish a settlement at Winyah Bay in 1526. Another colony established near Parrish Island by French Huguenots thirty six years later also failed, and it wasn't until 1670 that the first permanent settlement was established by the English at Albemarle Point.

The coastal swamps were favorable for the cultivation of rice, made profitable by the use of slave labor, and soon the region was flourishing. Other Europeans, namely Irish, Scottish, German, and Welsh flocked to the southern part of the new province, while inland areas continued to develop. Generally the settlers were on friendly terms with the Native American population, though there was a small uprising of Yamasee in 1715, fueled by Spanish colonists at St. Augustine, which was successfully put down.

South Carolina, due to the original grant by the Crown, was an exceptionally large colony, so it was soon divided into the two separate provinces of North Carolina and Georgia. This division sealed South Carolina's fate to become a relatively small state. The colonists successfully overturned the rule of the original proprietors in 1719, and the Crown assumed control of the government on 1721.

The area was an unsettled one, and skirmishes with the Indians, Spanish, French and pirates, and a slave uprising in 1739, defined the pre-Revolutionary period. South Carolina played an active role in the American Revolution after opposing the Stamp Act in 1765, and Fort Charlotte in McCormick County was the first property seized by Revolutionary forces in 1775. Leaders from South Carolina took an active part in the federal constitution convention in 1787, and South Carolina became the eighth state to ratify the constitution on May 23, 1788.

Taxes and slavery were the main issues in the state in the period between the Revolutionary and Civil Wars, and though able to compromise on taxes with the federal government, there was no such give with the subject of slavery. When South Carolina seceded from the union in 1860, more than half the population of the state were black slaves.

The Civil War erupted in South Carolina at Fort Sumter on April 12, 1861. The Sea Islands were quickly captured by Union forces, but Charleston withstood a long and relentless siege until February 1865. Columbia was burned by General Sherman and his troops towards the end of the war, and the state experienced widespread destruction throughout. Over 60,000 soldiers from South Carolina fought for the Confederacy during the Civil War, with close to 14,000 killed in battle or dying while in capture.

South Carolina was occupied by Union troops following the war, and the Reconstruction era saw the state plunged into debt. This situation led a revision of the state constitution and at a convention in 1868 where black representatives outnumbered whites by 76:48, the first significant political gains of blacks, namely the positions of US representative and lieutenant governor occurred.

Political representation of blacks was unpopular with white militants, known as Red Shirts, who rode through the countryside urging white voters to back the gubernatorial candidacy of former Confederate General Wade Hampton. Hampton won the election, but was restrained from taking office by the Republican incumbent until President Rutherford B. Hayes declared an end to Reconstruction and began the withdrawal of federal troops from the state in April 1877.

Important Dates in South Carolina History

1663 – Area granted to eight proprietors

1669 – Fundamental constitution of the colony devised

1706 – Province divided into twelve parishes

1712 – Carolina divided into two provinces

1715 – Yamasee uprising

1719 – Becomes a Royal colony

1780 – British forces occupy Charleston

1781 – Battle of Cowpens

1782 – British evacuate Charleston

1860 – Secedes from Union

1861 – Fort Sumter attacked

1865 – Union troops take Charleston

1865 – Union troops burn Columbia

1868 – Readmitted to Union

Famous Battles Fought in South Carolina

Among the many battles fought in South Carolina during the Revolutionary War were the major Patriot victories at Ft. Moultrie in the **Battle of Sullivan's Island** in1776, the **Battle of Kings Mountain**, in 1780, and the **Battle of Cowpens** in 1781.

The first battle of the Civil War, the **Battle of Fort Sumter**, took place in South Carolina, bombardment of the Union stronghold beginning on April 7, 1863. The **Battle of Fort Wagner** at Morris Island was a bloody affair resulting in a Confederate victory, while other engagements of note took place at **Honey Hill** in 1864 and **River's Bridge** in 1865.

These battle accounts that exist can be very effective in uncovering the military records of your ancestor. They can tell you what regiments fought in which battles, and often include the names and ranks of many officers and enlisted men.

Battle of Sullivan's Island: http://totallyhistory.com/battle-of-sullivans-island/

Battle of Kings Mountain:http://www.revolutionarywararchives.org/kingsmtfall05.html

Battle of Cowpens: http://www.nps.gov/cowp/historyculture/the-battle-of-cowpens.htm

Battle of Fort Sumter:
http://www.nps.gov/hps/abpp/battles/sc001.htm

Battle of Fort Wagner:
http://www.nps.gov/hps/abpp/battles/sc007.htm

Honey Hill: http://www.nps.gov/hps/abpp/battles/sc010.htm

River's Bridge: http://www.nps.gov/hps/abpp/battles/sc011.htm

Common South Carolina Genealogical Issues and Resources to Overcome Them

Boundary Changes: Boundary changes are a common obstacle when researching South Carolina ancestors. You could be searching for an ancestor's record in one county when in fact it is stored in a different one due to historical county boundary changes.

The **Atlas of Historical County Boundaries** can help you to overcome that problem. It provides a chronological listing of every boundary change that has occurred in the history of South Carolina.

Atlas of Historical County Boundaries link to: http://publications.newberry.org/ahcbp/documents/SC_Consolidated _Chronology.htm#Consolidated_Chronology

Name Changes: Surname changes, variations, and misspellings can complicate genealogical research. It is important to check all spelling variations. Soundex, a program that indexes names by sound, is a useful first step, but you can't rely on it completely as some name variations result in different Soundex codes. The surnames could be different, but the first name may be different too. You can also find records filed under initials, middle names, and nicknames as well, so you will need to **get creative with surname variations** and spellings in order to cover all the possibilities. For help with surname variations read our instructional article on **How to Use Soundex**.

get creative with surname variations: http://obituarieshelp.org/blog/?p=634

How to Use Soundex: http://obituarieshelp.org/blog/?p=505

South Carolina Genealogical Organizations and Archives

Genealogical resources include not only records, but the organizations that house them, or can direct you to them. These institutions include: *Archives, Libraries, Genealogical Societies, Family History Centers, Universities, Churches, and Museums.*

Following are links to their websites, their physical addresses, and a summary of the records you can find there.

Archives and Libraries

South Carolina Department of Archives and History - census records, county probate records, county land records, county equity court records, military records, and state death certificates.

8301 Parklane Road
Columbia, SC 29229
Telephone: 803-896-6100
Fax: 803-896-6198

South Carolina Department of Archives and History:
http://archives.sc.gov/recordsheld/Pages/GenealogyResources.aspx

National Archives Southeast Region (Atlanta) - South Carolina citizenship applications, slave manifests, South Carolina military records, Federal census, 1790-1930, Slave censuses 1850 and 1860, Freedmens Bureau records, Dawes Commission Final Cards for Cherokee, Choctaw, Chickasaw, Creek, and Seminole Tribes, Atlantic Ports Passenger Arrivals

5780 Jonesboro Road
Morrow, GA 30260
Telephone: 770-968-2100
Fax: 770-968-2547

National Archives Southeast Region (Atlanta):
http://www.archives.gov/atlanta/public/services.html#genealogy

Greenville County Library System - Newspaper, Obituary, Marriage, and Vital records indexes

Greenville County Library System:
http://www.greenvillelibrary.org/index.php/research/genealogy

Laurens County Public Library - Census Records on Microfilm SC for 1790 – 1930, Military Records: American Revolution, Civil War & WW I and II; SC Death Certificate Index on Microfiche: 1915-1924, 1925-1934, 1935-1949, Will & Estates Records for Laurens County: 1785-1900, DAR Lineage Books and Cemetery Records,Local Newspapers:Laurens Advertiser beginning 1885; Laurensville Herald June 1845 to July 1929 (incomplete); Clinton Chronicle recent years, Maps, Family Histories, Bible & Church Records

1017 West Main Street
Laurens, South Carolina 29360
Tel: (864) 681-7323
Fax: (864) 681-0598

Laurens County Public Library: http://www.lcpl.org/genealogy/

Charleston County Public Library - Vital records, Wills, Immigration records, Land and Tax records, Military records, City Directories, Historical resources

68 Calhoun Street
Charleston, SC 29401
Phone: (843) 805-6930
Fax: (843) 727-3741

Charleston County Public Library·
http://www.ccpl.org/content.asp?catID=6078&parentID=

South Carolina Genealogical and Historical Societies

Genealogical and historical societies have access to extensive catalogues of genealogical data. They are also able to offer expert guidance for genealogical researchers. Many members are professional genealogists who are most willing to share their expertise in finding ancestors.

South Carolina Historical Society – naturalizations, county census records and mortality schedules, church records, vital records, immigration records and passenger lists, manuscripts, historical newspapers,

100 Meeting Street
Charleston, SC 29401-2299
Telephone: 803-723-3225
Fax: 803-723-8584

South Carolina Historical Society:
http://www.southcarolinahistoricalsociety.org/

South Carolina Genealogical Society – county histories, cemetery records, surname directory, and miscellaneous genealogy resources

PO Box 24526
Columbia, SC 29224

South Carolina Genealogical Society: http://www.scgen.org/

African American Historical Alliance - Civil War and Reconstruction Era resources
636-G Long Point Road, Box 32
Mount Pleasant, SC 29464
info@aahasc.org
(843) 216-5790 Fax

African American Historical Alliance:
http://www.aahasc.org/about/

Additional South Carolina Genealogy Resources

South Carolina Mailing Lists

Mailing lists are internet based facilities that use email to distribute a single message to all who subscribe to it. When information on a particular surname, new records, or any other important genealogy information related to the mailing list topic becomes available, the subscribers are alerted to it. Joining a mailing list is an excellent way to stay up to date on South Carolina genealogy research topics. Rootsweb have an extensive listing of **South Carolina Mailing Lists** on a variety of topics.

South Carolina Mailing Lists:
http://lists.rootsweb.ancestry.com/index/usa/SC/misc.html

South Carolina Message Boards

A message board is another internet based facility where people can post questions about a specific genealogy topic and have it answered by other genealogists. If you have questions about a surname, record type, or research topic, you can post your question and other researchers and genealogists will help you with the answer. Be sure to check back regularly, as the answers are not emailed to you. The **South Carolina** message boards at **Rootsweb** are completely free to use.

Rootsweb:
http://boards.rootsweb.com/localities.northam.usa.states.southcarolina/mb.ashx

South Carolina Newspapers and Periodicals

Many genealogy periodicals and historical newspapers contain reprinted copies of family genealogies, transcripts of family Bible records, information about local records and archives, census indexes, church records, queries, land records, obituaries, court records, cemetery records, and wills. The following sites have historical South Carolina newspapers and periodicals that you can search online or on-site.

South Carolina Department of Archives and History – historical newspapers and periodicals from 17th and 18th centuries

8301 Parklane Road
Columbia, SC 29229
Telephone: 803-896-6100
Fax: 803-896-6198

South Carolina Department of Archives and History:
http://archives.sc.gov/recordsheld/Pages/GenealogyResources.aspx

GenealogyBank.com – free searchable database of South Carolina newspaper archives, 1783–1970

GenealogyBank.como:
http://www.genealogybank.com/gbnk/newspapers/explore/USA/South_Carolina/

The Online Books Page – links to historical South Carolina books and periodicals available for viewing online

The Online Books Page:
http://onlinebooks.library.upenn.edu/webbin/book/browse?type=subject&c=c&key=south+carolina

Library of Congress Digital Newspaper Directory – free searchable database of historical U.S. newspapers dating from 1690-present

Library of Congress Digital Newspaper Directory: http://chroniclingamerica.loc.gov/search/titles/

NewspaperArchive.com – largest online database of historical newspapers in the world.

NewspaperArchive.com: http://newspaperarchive.com/

Historical South Carolina Maps and Gazetteers

Maps are an integral part of genealogical research. They help us to locate landmarks, towns, cities, parishes, states, provinces, waterways and roads and streets. They also help us to determine when and where boundary changes might have taken place, and give us a visualization of the area we're researching in.

For locating place names, a gazetteer is the best possible resource for any genealogist. Gazetteers are also sometimes called "place name dictionaries", and can help you to locate the area in which you need to conduct research. Below are links to the maps and gazetteers for research in South Carolina.

Peabody GNIS Service – South Carolina link to: http://peabody.research.yale.edu/cgi-bin/Query.GNIS?ST=South%20Carolina&SU=1

Color Landform Atlas – South Carolina link to: http://fermi.jhuapl.edu/states/sc_0.html

1985 U.S. Atlas link to: http://www.livgenmi.com/1895/SC/

South Carolina Hometown Locator link to: http://southcarolina.hometownlocator.com/

South Carolina City Directories
.

City directories are similar to telephone directories in that they list the residents of a particular area. The difference though is what is important to genealogists, and that is they pre-date telephone directories. You can find an ancestor's information such as their street address, place of employment, occupation, or the name of their spouse. A one-stop-shop for finding city directories in South Carolina is the **South Carolina Online Historical Directories** which contains a listing of every available online historical directory related to South Carolina.

South Carolina Online Historical Directories:
https://sites.google.com/site/onlinedirectorysite/Home/usa/sc

South Carolina Historical Society – City directories for Charleston, South Carolina for the years 1803, 1806, 1807, 1809, and 1813, city directories for Columbia 1902-1935

100 Meeting Street
Charleston, SC 29401-2299
Telephone: 803-723-3225
Fax: 803-723-8584

South Carolina Historical Society:
http://www.southcarolinahistoricalsociety.org/

South Carolina Genealogical Records

Birth, Death, Marriage and Divorce Records – Also known as vital records, birth, death, and marriage certificates are the most basic, yet most important records attached to your ancestor. The reason for their importance is that they not only place your ancestor in a specific place at a definite time, but potentially connect the individual to other relatives. Below is a list of repositories and websites where you can find South Carolina vital records. South Carolina did not issue birth and death certificates prior to January 1, 1915. Early vital records were kept by some of the larger cities and are available from the appropriate county health department, except for a few major cities where the records are at the city health department. For vital records after 1915 you can write to:

Office of Vital Records and Public Health Statistics
2600 Bull Street
Columbia, SC 29201
Telephone: 803-734-4830
Fax: 803-799-0301

Some early vital records for South Carolina can be found at:

South Carolina Historical Society – Union County, South Carolina, marriage records : from early newspapers, 1851-1912, marriage register, Spartanburg County marriages, 1785-191, York County marriages, 1770-1869, Records of births and deaths in the City of Charleston, 1821-1926, county birth registers, Death and marriage notices from the Watchman and Observer, 1845-1855 , Edgefield marriage records, from the late 18th century up through 1870 , Charleston, South Carolina marriages, 1877-1895, various county marriage records 1643 to mid twentieth century

100 Meeting Street
Charleston, SC 29401-2299
Telephone: 803-723-3225
Fax: 803-723-8584

South Carolina Historical Society:
http://www.southcarolinahistoricalsociety.org/

Family Search has the following indexes which can be searched online for free:

South Carolina Births and Christenings, 1681-1935:
https://familysearch.org/search/collection/1675535

South Carolina Deaths, 1915-1943:
https://familysearch.org/search/collection/1417492

South Carolina Deaths, 1944-1955:
https://familysearch.org/search/collection/1589507

South Carolina Marriages, 1709-1913:
https://familysearch.org/search/collection/1675541

South Carolina Census Reports

Census records are among the most important genealogical documents for placing your ancestor in a particular place at a specific time. Like BDM records, they can also lead you to other ancestors, particularly those who were living under the authority of the head of household.

Federal census records for South Carolina exist from 1790 –1930 and can be found at:

South Carolina Department of Archives and History - Federal Census Records 1790-1930

8301 Parklane Road
Columbia, SC 29229
Telephone: 803-896-6100
Fax: 803-896-6198

South Carolina Department of Archives and History:
http://archives.sc.gov/recordsheld/Pages/GenealogyResources.aspx

National Archives Southeast Region (Atlanta) - South Federal census, 1790-1930, Slave censuses 1850 and 1860, Freedmens Bureau records

5780 Jonesboro Road
Morrow, GA 30260
Telephone: 770-968-2100
Fax: 770-968-2547

National Archives Southeast Region (Atlanta) :
http://www.archives.gov/atlanta/public/services.html#genealogy

South Carolina Historical Society – Individual county census records and mortality schedules, 1790-1860

100 Meeting Street
Charleston, SC 29401-2299
Telephone: 803-723-3225
Fax: 803-723-8584
South Carolina Historical Society:
http://www.southcarolinahistoricalsociety.org/

The **Free Census Project** has transcribed many South Carolina indexes and new material is added daily

Free Census Project: http://usgwcensus.org/cenfiles/sc.htm

Access Genealogy – South Carolina county census records dating from 1790

Access Genealogy: http://www.accessgenealogy.com/census/south-carolina-census-records.htm

African American Census Schedules Online – slave schedules, mortality schedules, slave-owners census

African American Census Schedules Online:
http://www.afrigeneas.com/aacensus/ga/

Native Americans in Census Records (US National Archives)

Native Americans in Census Records:
http://www.archives.gov/research/census/native-americans/

South Carolina Church Records

Church and synagogue records are a valuable resource, especially for baptisms, marriages, and burials that took place before 1900. You will need to at least have an idea of your ancestor's religious denomination, and in most cases you will have to visit a brick and mortar establishment to view them.

Most church records are kept by the individual church, although in some denominations, records are placed in a regional archive or maintained at the diocesan level. Local Historical Societies are sometimes the repository for the state's older church records. Below are links archives that maintain church records, as well as a few databases that can be viewed online.

The **Family History Library** contains many church records from a variety of denominations on microfilm.

Family History Library:
http://familysearch.org/learn/wiki/en/Family_History_Library

South Carolina Historical Society – Huge collection of church records from various denominations and individual churches dating from Colonial tomes

100 Meeting Street
Charleston, SC 29401-2299
Telephone: 803-723-3225
Fax: 803-723-8584

South Carolina Historical Society:
http://www.southcarolinahistoricalsociety.org/

Central Repositories for Denominational Records

Church of Jesus Christ of Latter-day Saints (Mormons)

Early Mormon Church records for South Carolina can be found on film located at the LDS Family History Library in Salt Lake City and can be searched via the **Family History Library Catalog**

Family History Library Catalog:
https://familysearch.org/eng/Library/FHLC/frameset_fhlc.asp

Baptist

South Carolina Baptist Historical Collection
James B. Duke Library
Furman University
3300 Poinsett Highway
Greenville, SouthCarolina 29613-0600
Phone: (864) 294-2194
Fax: (864) 294-2194

South Carolina Baptist Historical Collection:
http://library.furman.edu/specialcollections/baptist/baptist_resources.htm

Methodist

South Carolina Methodist Conference Archives
Sandor Teszler Library
Wofford College
429 N. Church Street
Spartanburg, SC 29301-3663
Phone: (864) 597-4300
Fax: (864) 597-4329

Sandor Teszler Library: http://www.wofford.edu/library/

<u>Presbyterian and Reformed</u>

Department of History-Montreat Presbyterian Church (U.S.A.)
318 Georgia Terrace
P.O. Box 849
Montreat, NC 28757
Phone: (704) 669-7061
Fax: (704) 669-5369

Department of History-Montreat Presbyterian Church:
http://www.phcmontreat.org/

<u>Roman Catholic</u>

Diocese of Charleston Archives
119 Broad Street
P.O. Box 818
Charleston, SC 29402
Phone: (803) 723-3488
Fax: (803) 724-6387

Diocese of Charleston Archives: http://sccatholic.org/archives-and-records-management

South Carolina Military Records

More than 40 million Americans have participated in some time of war service since America was colonized. The chance of finding your ancestor amongst those records is exceptionally high. Military records can even reveal individuals who never actually served, such as those who registered for the two World Wars but were never called to duty.

Below are a number of links to websites and archives that contain South Carolina military records.

South Carolina Department of Archives and History - Records of Confederate Soldiers Serving from South Carolina, 1861-1865, Compiled Service Records of Confederate General and Staff Officers and Non-regimental Enlisted Personnel, 1861-1865, Rolls of South Carolina Volunteers in the Confederate States Provisional Army, Roll of Honor Roll of Dead South Carolina Troops, Pension applications 1919-1925, Artificial Limb Applications and Vouchers, 1879-1899, Confederate Home and Infirmary Applications

8301 Parklane Road
Columbia, SC 29229
Telephone: 803-896-6100
Fax: 803-896-6198

South Carolina Department of Archives and History:
http://archives.sc.gov/recordsheld/Pages/GenealogyResources.aspx

US Department of Veterans Affairs Nationwide Gravesite Locator – includes information on veterans and their family members buried in veterans and military cemeteries having a government grave marker.

US Department of Veterans Affairs Nationwide Gravesite Locator: http://gravelocator.cem.va.gov/

You may also find your ancestor's military records in the following databases:

United States General Index to Pension Files, 1861-1934

United States General Index to Pension Files, 1861-1934: https://familysearch.org/search/collection/1919699

United States Index to Service Records, War with Spain, 1898

United States Index to Service Records, War with Spain, 1898: https://familysearch.org/search/collection/1919583

United States Index to Indian Wars Pension Files, 1892-1926 – military pension records of soldiers who fought in the Indian Wars between 1817 and 1898

United States Index to Indian Wars Pension Files, 1892-1926: https://familysearch.org/search/collection/1979427

United States Registers of Enlistments in the U.S. Army, 1798-1914 - index of men who enlisted in the United States Army, 1798-1914.

United States Registers of Enlistments in the U.S. Army, 1798-1914: https://familysearch.org/search/collection/1880762

United States Mexican War Pension Index, 1887-1926 - index to Mexican War pension files for service between 1846 and 1848

United States Mexican War Pension Index, 1887-1926: https://familysearch.org/search/collection/1979390

Civil War Soldiers Service Records - Service records for both Union and Confederate soldiers indexed by soldier's name, rank, and unit.

Civil War Soldier Service Records: http://go.fold3.com/civilwar_records/

South Carolina Cemetery Records

As convenient as it is to search cemetery records online, keep in mind that there are a few disadvantages over visiting a cemetery in person. They are:

- Tombstone information is not always accurately transcribed
- The arrangement of the graves in a cemetery can be crucial as family members are often buried next to each other or in the same grave. This arrangement is not always preserved in the alphabetical indexes that are found online.

With that information in mind, the following websites have databases that can be searched online for South Carolina Cemetery records.

South Carolina Genealogical Society – S.C. Cemetery GPS Mapping Project

PO Box 24526
Columbia, SC 29224

South Carolina Genealogical Society: http://www.gps.scgen.org/

South Carolina Tombstone Transcription Project - death and burial records

South Carolina Tombstone Transcription Project:
http://www.usgwtombstones.org/southcarolina/scarolina.html

African American Cemeteries Online – African American, slave, and Native American cemetery records

African American Cemeteries Online:
http://africanamericancemeteries.com/ar/

Access Genealogy – database of South Carolina cemetery record transcriptions

Access Genealogy: http://www.accessgenealogy.com/cemetery/south-carolina-cemetery-records.htm

Find a Grave – over 100 million grave records can be searched on this site. Search can be conducted by name, location, or cemetery name.

Find a Grave: http://www.findagrave.com/

Interment.net - A free online database containing approximately 4 million cemetery records from around the world.

Interment.net: http://www.interment.net/

Billion Graves – as the name implies, you can search a billion records including headstone photos, transcriptions, cemetery records, and grave locations.

Billion Graves : http://billiongraves.com/pages/search/index.php#cemetery

South Carolina Obituaries

Obituaries can reveal a wealth about our ancestor and other relatives. You can search our **South Carolina Obituaries Listings** from hundreds of South Carolina newspapers online for free.

South Carolina Obituaries Listings: http://obituarieshelp.org/south_carolina_newspaper_obituaries.html

South Carolina Wills and Probate Records

The documents found in a probate packet may include a complete inventory of a person's estate, newspaper entries, witness testimony, a copy of a will, list of debtors and creditors, names of executors or trustees, names of heirs. They can not only tell you about the ancestor you're currently researching, but lead to other ancestors.

South Carolina Department of Archives and History - County Wills 1671-1868, Will Transcripts 1782-1855

8301 Parklane Road
Columbia, SC 29229
Telephone: 803-896-6100
Fax: 803-896-6198

South Carolina Department of Archives and History:
http://archives.sc.gov/recordsheld/Pages/GenealogyResources.aspx

South Carolina Historical Society – Marion County probate records, Williamsburg County probate records, 1806-ca. 1900

100 Meeting Street
Charleston, SC 29401-2299
Telephone: 803-723-3225
Fax: 803-723-8584

South Carolina Historical Society:
http://www.southcarolinahistoricalsociety.org/

Family Search has the following indexes that can be searched online for free:

South Carolina Probate Records, Bound Volumes, 1671-1977:
https://familysearch.org/search/collection/1919417

South Carolina Probate Records, Files and Loose Papers, 1732-1964: https://familysearch.org/search/collection/1911928

South Carolina Immigration and Naturalization Records

The naturalization process generated many types of records, including petitions, declarations of intention, and oaths of allegiance. These records can provide family historians with information such as a person's birth date and place of birth, immigration year, marital status, spouse information, occupation, witnesses' names and addresses, and more.

South Carolina Historical Society – South Carolina naturalizations, 1783-1850, Naturalizations of foreign Protestants from 1869, Passneger and immigration lists

100 Meeting Street
Charleston, SC 29401-2299
Telephone: 803-723-3225
Fax: 803-723-8584

South Carolina Historical Society:
http://www.southcarolinahistoricalsociety.org/

National Archives Southeast Region (Atlanta) - South Carolina citizenship applications, Atlantic Ports Passenger Arrivals

5780 Jonesboro Road
Morrow, GA 30260
Telephone: 770-968-2100
Fax: 770-968-2547

National Archives Southeast Region (Atlanta):
http://www.archives.gov/atlanta/public/services.html#genealogy

South Carolina Native American Records

National Archives Southeast Region (Atlanta) - Dawes Commission Final Cards for Cherokee, Choctaw, Chickasaw, Creek, and Seminole Tribes

5780 Jonesboro Road
Morrow, GA 30260
Telephone: 770-968-2100
Fax: 770-968-2547

National Archives Southeast Region (Atlanta):
http://www.archives.gov/atlanta/public/services.html#genealogy

Access Genealogy – South Carolina Native American census records, tribal histories, and much more

Access Genealogy: http://www.accessgenealogy.com/native/south-carolina-indian-tribes.htm

U.S. National Archives - information on American Indians who maintained their ties to Federally-recognized Tribes (1830-1970).

U.S. National Archives: http://www.archives.gov/research/native-americans/

Records of the Bureau of Indian Affairs (BIA)

Records of the Bureau of Indian Affairs (BIA):
http://www.archives.gov/research/guide-fed-records/groups/075.html

American Indians Records Repository - records dating from the 1700s including trust, education and other historic Indian Affairs records

American Indian Records Repository
Meritex Enterprises
17501 West 98th Street
Lenexa, KS 66219
Phone: 913-888-0601

American Indians Records Repository:
http://www.doi.gov/ost/records_mgmt/american-indian-records-repository.cfm

Missing Matriarchs – Resources for Researching Female South Carolina Ancestors

Looking for female ancestors requires an adjustment of how we view traditional records sources. A woman's identity was often under that of her husband, and often individual records for them can be difficult to locate. The following resources are effective in locating female ancestors in South Carolina where traditional records may not reveal them.

Bibliographies

- *South Carolina Women,* Idella Bodie (Sandlapper Publishing, 1978)
- *Mill and Town in South Carolina, 1880-1920,* David Carlton (Louisiana State University Press, 1982)
- *Carolina Families: A Bibliography of Books About North and South Carolina Families,* Donald M. Hehir (Heritage Books, 1994)
- *A Hard Fight for We: Women's Transition from Slavery to Freedom in South Carolina,* Leslie A. Schwalm (University of Illinois Press, 1997)

Selected Resources for South Carolina Women's History

Association of Black Women Historians
Department of History
South Carolina State University
Orangeburg, SC 29117

Ida Jane Dacus Library
Winthrop College
Oakland Avenue
Rock Hill, SC 29733

Common South Carolina Surnames

The following surnames are among the most common in South Carolina and are also being currently researched by other genealogists. If you find your surname here, there is a chance that some research has already been performed on your ancestor.

Abercrombie, Adair, Adams, Alewine, Anderson, Armstrong, Arnald, Arnold, Ashley, Atkin, Bagwell, Baker, Baldwin, Banister, Bannister, Barbara, Barker, Batson, Baynard, Bayne, Beason, Beaty, Bertha, Betty, Bigby, Bishop, Blackwell, Bleman, Bohle, Boiter, Bowyer, Bramlett, Bramlette, Brissey, Broadway, Brock, Brook, Brooks, Broome, Brown, Brunson, Bryant, Bryson, Buchanan, Buggew, Bullock, Burch, Burdette, Burgess, Burke, Burrell, Callaham, Campbell, Capps, Carter, Case, Casey, Chabra, Chambers, Chandler, Chapman, Chastain, Chasteen, Clamp, Clardy, Clark, Classen, Cleveland, Cobb, Coffee, Coker, Collins, Conn, Cooley, Cothran, Cousins, Cox, Craine, Crawford, Crowe, Croy, Crumley, Curtis, Darby, Davenport, Davidson, Davis, Dean, Dominick, Downes, Downs, Driggers, Duncan, Dunlap, Dunn, Durham, Eads, Elgin, Ellingburg, Erickson, Erwin, Eskew, Ester, Etris, Evans, Evelyn, Farmer, Faye, Ficklin, Fields, Finch, Findley, Flicker, Ford, Fortson, Fowler, Franks, Freeman, Fullbright, Fuller,Gambrell, Garrett, Gay, Gentry, George, Gilreath, Gossett, Graham, Greene, Gregory, Grumbles, Gunnels, Hammonds, Hand, Hanna, Hansen, Harper, Harris, Harrison, Hatcher, Hembree, Henderson, Henry, Herlong, Hill, Hillhouse, Hills, Holcombe, Holley, Holliday, Hollingsworth, Hood, Hooper, Hopkins, Howard, Howell, Hudson, Hunter, Hutchinson, Ivey, Ivie, Jackson, Jenkins, Johnny, Johnson, Katherine, Kay, Keeler, Keesler, Keitt, Kelly, Kennemore, King, Kissimon, Kizian, Knight, Knox, Kutch, Lambert, Landress, Larkin, Leathers, Leopard, Lewis, Linch, Lindley, Lingford, Little, Littlefield, Livingston, Lollis, Louise, Mackey, Madden, Maddox, Mahr, Manning, Margie, Marie, Marlar, Martin, Mayfield, McBride, McClain, McColough, McCombs, McConnel, McCoy, McCuen, McDaniel, McGaha, McKee, McKellar, Medlin, Merch, Merle, Middleton, Miller, Minnie, Mize, Moon, Moore, Morgan, Mullinax, Murphy, Nance, Neely, Nickels, Norman,

Ogle, Oliver, Outs, Outz, Owens, Pace, Padgett, Page, Parker, Parsons, Patterson, Patton, Payne, Payton, Peden, Perry, Phillips, Pilgram, Poole, Poore, Powell, Pruitt, Ramey, Rankin, Rasmussen, Reed, Reeves, Rena, Rhodes, Ridge, Ridley, Roberts, Robertson, Robinson, Rochester, Rodgers, Rodrigriezs, Rogers, Rooker, Rooten, Ross, Ruth, Rutledge, Ryels, S, Sara, Sarah, Saville, Scott, Sears, Seggers, Seymour, Sinclair, Smith, South, Southern, Spivey, Staton, Stevens, Stone, Stowe, Strickland, Stringer, Tammy, Taylor, Thomas, Thompson, Tollet, Tollison, Trantham, Traynum, Tumblin, Tyner, Vaughn, Venzke, Vickery, Vincent, Vinson, Warren, Watkins, Westbrook, Whitaker, White, Whiten, Whitmore, William, Williams, Willis, Wilson, Winfree, Woehrle, Wolfe, Woodchuck, Woods, Woodson, Wooten, York, Young

About the Author

Gary L. Morris worked from 2009 to 2014 as a professional researcher for a major player in the genealogy field. After tracing his family lineage back to 1683, he has decided to publish these helpful guides to share the valuable information he has discovered during his career to help others trace their family lineages. An avid genealogist himself, he hopes you will find this guide factual, thorough, helpful, and most of all, effective in helping you to find your family members.

Made in the USA
Lexington, KY
07 April 2015